LOVE, LOVE, LOVE
The New Love Poetry

LOVE, LOVE, LOVE

The New Love Poetry

Edited with an Introduction
by
PETE ROCHE

CORGI BOOKS
A DIVISION OF TRANSWORLD PUBLISHERS

LOVE, LOVE, LOVE
A CORGI BOOK

PRINTING HISTORY
Corgi Edition published 1967
Corgi Edition reprinted 1968

552 07789 5

FG 7789

This book is set in
Bembo 11 pt.

Corgi Books are published by Transworld Publishers, Ltd.,
Bashley Road, London, N.W.10

Made and printed in Great Britain by
Richard Clay (The Chaucer Press), Ltd., Bungay, Suffolk

Acknowledgments

Peace is Milk, by Adrian Mitchell. Previously published in *Peace News*. Also published in *Out Loud* (Cape Goliard, 1967).

Stop Saying Oh, Oh, by Anselm Hollo. Previously published in *El Corno Emplumado* (Mexico City, 1966).

The Days: Air, by Anselm Hollo. Previously published in *Poetry* (Chicago, 1967).

Bear Love, by Anselm Hollo. Previously published in *I. Kon* (N.Y.C., 1967).

Direct Communication, by Michael Horovitz. Previously published in *Evergreen Review* (New York, 1965).

Dawning, by Michael Horovitz. Previously published in *Underdog* (Liverpool, 1966).

For My Wife and Chagall. Previously published in *Strangers* (New Departure, London, 1965).

For M, Loving You and Morning Waking all by Frances Horovitz. Previously published in *Aylesford Review Poets—1*.

I Only Kiss, Here's to the Girl and Hat, all by Alan Jackson. Previously published in *All Fall Down* (The Kevin Press, Edinburgh).

Edinburgh Scene, by Alan Jackson. Previously published in *The Worstest Beast* (Kevin Press, Edinburgh).

The White Stallion, by Pete Morgan. Previously published in *Festival Poetry*, 1966 (Gambit).

Springpoem in Glorious Colour, by Pete Brown. Previously published in *Underdog*.

Poem by Libby Houston. Previously published in *A Stained Glass Raree Show* (Allison & Busby, 1967).

The Train, by Paul Evans. Previously published in *Young Commonwealth Poets* (Heinemann).

A Praise for Rhiannon, by Paul Evans. Previously published in *The New British Poetry* (Poetmeat No. 8).

The Branches, by Paul Evans. Previously published in *Eleventh Finger*, No. 1.

Song of the Pink Bird, On a Horse Called Autumn, Party Piece, Song for a Last Year's Wife, and A Creature to Tell the Time By, all by Brian Patten. Previously published in *Little Johnny's Confession*, by Brian Patten (Allen & Unwin, 1966).

Conny, To My Unborn Child, Sandcastles Built to Smother You, and The Bodies are Touching, all by Tom Pickard. Previously published in *High on the Walls* (The Fulcrum Press, 1967).

Rain, Ice Age, and Love Story, all by Henry Graham. Previously published in *Ambit*.

Park Trip, by Maurice Cockrill. Previously published in *Matrix*.

Contents

Introduction

This collection differs from other anthologies in that this is the first occasion—so far as I know—that the work of so many young British poets has been collected together in one volume. There are thirty-one writers here in all, with an average age of around 25, and many of the poems are appearing in print for the first time.

I have confined my selection to the work of young writers not only because I feel that a representative selection of the poetry that is being written by today's young poets is a worthwhile venture in itself but also because I believe that their work represents a significant departure—both in style and content—from the kind of poetry that has been produced in this country over the last fifteen years or so.

Part of the reason for this lies in the feeling of impatience and general dissatisfaction which any generation almost inevitably has for its immediate literary predecessors; and it would certainly be true to say that many of the poets represented here feel a closer affinity with some of today's better pop lyricists than they do with most of the poets who were in vogue in the 'fifties and early 'sixties.

Far more influential, however, in producing this schism has been the recent increase in the popularity of poetry readings, particularly among younger people. The success in this respect of the Liverpool poets (all of whom are included here) and of what has been called The Great Liverpool Experiment have already been well documented. But this new interest in oral poetry is by no means confined to Merseyside: the readings organised by Tom Pickard in Newcastle, by Alan Jackson in Edinburgh, by Mike Horovitz and Pete Brown in London and the growing number of readings in other towns and cities throughout the country—all bear witness to the increasing demand for living poetry, poetry that talks to people in a direct and comprehensible way. It is no coincidence that virtually all of the poets in this book, when discussing their work, are quick to stress the value of these live performances.

And it is this quite novel situation—young poets reading their work to predominantly young audiences—that is giving the poetry of the mid-'sixties its distinctive character, is investing it (whatever faults in technique one may find in individual poems) with a vigour and a feeling for the realities of life that have been absent from English poetry for too long.

As far as the book's general theme is concerned, many of the poems here are poems about love rather than conventional 'love poems'; a reading of Adrian Mitchell's powerful argument for what might be termed Universal Love should give a fair indication of the width of scope which I've allowed myself. (Incidentally, my justification for including a few slightly older poets—like Mitchell, Horovitz and Henri—is that they have played a central part in demonstrating the possibilities of 'live' poetry to younger writers.)

Finally, I should like to thank the many people who made useful suggestions while this book was in progress, with a special word of thanks to Pete Brown, whose considerable help and encouragement have made my work a lot lighter.

PETE ROCHE

HENRY GRAHAM

A Bridge a Crossing

At morning there are flowers to cut the heart.
A bad time this to open one's eyes. I know it best
to wait the hot summers afternoon narcotic;
the silence, alien as your hair;
racemes of bright yellow flowers.

Lovely child, to cut open a heart requires training;
any hesitation, no matter how slight, kills;
and you live always with a sharp knife poised,
ready to prune away the dying meat of the rose.
When you eventually discard your intentions
I shall leave you for other gardens.

Rain

She said she liked the rain
sometimes. I, that the only thing
I have against it is it makes
you wet. Anyway on hot summer nights
the sound of it is cool. She said
when you are crossed in love
you listen to the words of songs.
I said that being in love is bad
of the stomach; no one
should be in love after thirty.
She kissed me and ran naked
out into the rain, and indigestion
burned inside me like a fire.

Four Love Poems After Reading the Chinese

1

This morning the sky is so leaden.
Catching sight of a seagull
through misted glass brings tears
to my eyes. And later
in the grey rain wet streets
the sight of a girl with
short hair stops me in my tracks.
I know that when I eventually
meet you, you will be cold to me,
and show me again the ring
given you by another.

2

When I hear that you have been
asking for me, even days
after, I look for you.
It is approaching the time of the
full moon and the tides are high.
The sound of your name releases
a flood of remembering.

3

Tonight I am drinking. The beer
is good, and the faces are all filled
with teeth: we all enjoy
the bright lights and the laughter.
Even I am laughing, though
the girl I am with asks
why I am so bitter.

4

I am depressed by the cold weather.
I know the winter will be
over soon, and I have not much
to say. Writing these words
is more like touching your arm.

Ice Age

I don't need you for anything in particular lately,
(my palms are burning
with an impatient fever to grasp glaciers)
and you seem to be evaporating.
You are all dried up darling,
about to doubt
your ability to turn into a small barren desert.
Don't do it. I will only
have to brush you up; and later
you will certainly get into my shoes,
irritating me once again.

Love Story

Not for nothing does your step
on the stair make me sit up,
stand even; go towards the door.
Your advent is always more
pleasurable than your presence.
I am aware that after the act
we both need to be somewhere else.
Cambodia isn't such a bad place, they
look happy, seem to believe in
something, though I have only
seen them in black and white.

You dress far too quickly for my
liking. Not for nothing do I ask you
to believe in what I say. You never listen.
Concerned with hooks and eyes
your fingers remind me of the girls
in the paddy fields separating
the new rice shoots. They too
would wish to be somewhere else;
not knee deep in warm muddy water.

Nothing for not loving I suppose
is the result of struggling in a bed
of warm muddy water. It always
amazes me how adept you are at getting
into those impossible garments, how
easily you fasten together your excuses for
leaving at once; and how sad your eyes look.
Just about now you would be laying aside
the young rice shoots, straightening
your back, looking at the sun low in the
sky and thinking of your new husband.

ADRIAN MITCHELL

Peace is Milk

Peace is milk.
War is acid.
The elephant dreams of bathing in lakes of milk.
Acid blood
Beats through the veins
Of the monstrous, vulture-weight fly,
Shaking, rocking his framework.

The elephants, their gentle thinking shredded
By drugs disseminated in the electricity supply,
Sell their children, buy tickets for the Zoo
And form a dead-eyed queue
Which stretches from the decorative, spiked gates
To the enormous shed where the flies are perching.

Peace is milk.
War is acid.
Sometimes an elephant finds a bucket of milk.
SWASH! and it's empty.
The fly feeds continually.
The fly bulges with acid
Or he needs more. And more.

An overweight fly levers himself
From his revolving chair,
Paces across the elephantskin floor,
Presses a button
And orders steak, steak, elephant steak
And a pint of acid.

Peace is milk.
War is acid.
The elephants are being dried in the sun.
The huge flies overflow.

Look down from the plane.
Those clouds of marvellous milk.
Easily they swing by on the wind,
Assembling, disassembling,
Forming themselves into pleasure-towers,
Unicorns, waterfalls, funny faces;
Swimming, basking, dissolving—
Easily, easily.

Tomorrow the cream-clouds will be fouled.
The sky will be buckshot-full of paratroop swarms
With their money-talking guns,
Headlines carved across their foreheads,
Sophisticated, silent electrical equipment,
Heart-screws and fear-throwers.
The day after tomorrow
The clouds will curdle, the clouds will begin to burn—
Yes, we expected that, knew about that,
Overkill, overburn, multi-megacorpse,
Yeah, yeah, yeah we knew about that,
Cry the white-hearted flies.

Channel One—
A fly scientist in an ivory helmet
Who always appears about to cry
Explains why the viewers have to die.

Channel Nine—
A fly statesman,
Hardly audible through the acid rain,
Explains why nothing can ever happen again.

Oh we'll soon be finished with the creatures of the earth.
There's no future in elephants, milk or Asiatics.
We should be working out
How to inflict the maximum pain
On Martians and Venusians.

Sour sky.
The elephants are entering the shed.
Sour sky.
The flies have dropped a star called Wormwood
And turned the Pacific into an acid bath.
Sour sky.
Socrates said no harm could come to a good man,
But even Socrates
Couldn't turn the hemlock into a banana milk-shake
With one high-voltage charge
From his Greek-sky eyes.
Even Socrates, poor bugger.

They are rubbing their forelegs together,
Washing each others' holes with their stubbled tongues,
Watching us while they wash.
Then, like brown rain running backwards,
They hurtle upwards, vibrating with acid.
They patrol our ceilings, always looking downwards.
Pick up the phone, that's them buzzing,
The turd-born flies.

Peace is milk
And milk is simple
And milk is hard to make.
It takes clean grass, fed by clean earth, clean air, clean rain,
Takes a calm cow with all her stomachs working
And it takes milk to raise that cow.

The milk is not for the good elephant.
The milk is not for the bad elephant.
But the milk may be for the lucky elephant
Looming along until the end of the kingdom of the flies.

A family of people, trapped in Death Valley,
Drank from the radiator,
Laid out hubcaps as bowls for the dew,
Buried each other up to the neck in sand
And waited for better times, which came
Just after they stopped hoping.

So the sweet survival of the elephants demands
Vision, cunning, energy and possibly burial
Until, maybe, the good times roll for the first time
And a tidal wave of elephants,
A stampede of milk,
Tornadoes through the capitals of flydom,
Voices flow like milk,
And below the white, nourishing depths—
Bodies moving any way they want to move,
Eyes resting or dancing at will,
Limbs and minds which follow, gladly,
The music of the milk.

You drink my milk, I'll drink yours,
We'll melt together in the sun
Despite the high-explosive flies
Which hover, which hover,
Which hover, which hover
Like a million plaguey Jehovahs.
Their prisons, their police, their armies, their laws,
Their camps where Dobermanns pace the cadaver of a field,
Their flame factories and Black Death factories,
The sourness of their sky—
That's the poisonous weather the elephants must lumber
                                                    through,

Surviving, surviving
Until the good times roll for the first time.

But it doesn't end
With an impregnable city carved out of the living light.
It doesn't end
In the plastic arms of an Everest-size Sophia Loren.
It doesn't end
When the world says a relieved farewell to the white man
As he goofs off to colonise the Milky Way.

It continues, it continues.
When all of the elephants push it goes slowly forward.
When they stop pushing it rolls backwards.
It continues, it continues
Towards milk, towards acid.

The taste of milk has been forgotten.
Most elephants agree peace is impossible.
Choosing death instead, they are jerked towards death
Slowly by newspapers, nightmares or cancer,
More quickly by heroin or war.
And some, the tops of their skulls sliced off
By money-knives or the axes of guilt,
Bow their great heads and let their hurting brains
Slop in the lavatory to drown.

There are prophets—grand-children of William Blake—
Desperate elephants who drink a pint of diamonds.
Their eyes become scored with a thousand white trenches,
Their hide shines with a constellation
Of diamond-headed boils,
Each footstep leaves a pool of diamond dust.
And sure, they shine,
They become shouting stars.
Burning with light until they are changed by pain
Into diamonds for everyone.

Sure, they go down shining,
They shine themselves to death,
The diamond drinkers.

The world is falling to pieces
But some of the pieces taste good.

There are various ways of making peace,
Most of them too childish for English elephants.
Given time and love it's possible
To cultivate a peace-field large enough
For the playing of a child.
It's possible to prepare a meal
And give it with care and love
To someone who takes it with care and love.
These are beginnings, but it's late, late—
TV Dinner tonight.
It's possible to suck the taste of peace
From one blade of grass
Or recognise peace in a can of white paint,
But it's not enough.
In Nirvana there's only room for one at a time.

WELL, YOU COULD STOP KILLING PEOPLE FOR A START.

Let loose the elephants.
Let the fountains talk milk.
Free the grass, let it walk wherever it likes.
Let the passports and prisons burn, their smoke turning into
milk.
Let the pot-smokers blossom into milk-coloured mental
petals.

We all need to be breast-fed
And start again.

Tear the fly-woven lying suits
Off the backs of the white killers
And let their milky bodies
Make naked pilgrimage
To wash the sores of Africa and Asia
With milk, for milk is peace
And money tastes of guns,
Guns taste of acid.

Make love well, generously, deeply.
There's nothing simpler in the savage world,
Making good love, making good good love.
There's nothing harder in the tender world,
Making good love, making good good love.
Most of the elephants, most of the time
Go starving for good love, not knowing what the pain is,
But it can be done and thank Blake it is done,
Making good love, making good good love.
In houses built of fly-turds, in fly-turd feasting mansions,
Fly-fear insurance offices even,
Fly-worshipping cathedrals even,
Even in murder offices just off the corridors of fly-power—
Making good love, making good good love.

Good lovers float,
Happy to know they are becoming real.
They float out and above the sourness, high on the seeds of
                                                    peace.
There are too few of them up there.
Too little milk.
Drink more milk.
Breed more cows and elephants.
Think more milk and follow your banana.
We need evangelist, door-to-door lovers,
Handing it out, laying it down,
Spreading the elephant seed, delivering the revolutionary
                                                    milk,

Making good love, making good good love.
United Nations teams of roving elephant milkmen
Making good love, making good good love,
Because peace is milk,
Peace is milk
And the skinny, thirsty earth, its face covered with flies,
Screams like a baby.

ADRIAN HENRI

Country Song

'Lily of the Valley' (Convallaria Majalis, fam. Lilliaceae).
Grows wild in N. England. Commonly cultivated.
Flowers in May. Berries red when ripe. Leaves particularly poisonous because three constituents depress the
heart, like Foxglove.

What are the constituents that depress the heart?
the scent of lilies in darkgreen silences under trees
milkweed and ragwort and sunshine in hedges
small flowers picked amongst trees when it's raining

A year ago
You planted lilies in the valley of my mind
There were lilies at the bottom of my garden
And ferrys at the bottom of my street

Now
I sit here in sunlight with the smell of wild garlic
Trying to taperecord the sound of windflowers and celandines

Wondering
What are the three constituents that depress the heart
Without you here in the country?

Love Story

You keep our love hidden
like the nightdress you keep under your pillow
and never wear when I'm there

But
one sunfilled day
you took me to your magic room
at the end of the yellow corridor
and showed me enchanted still-lifes
Niveatins BodyMist sprays coldcream jars
glowing like jewels
your body singing pink in the sunlight
opening to me like the red pulsing heart of a flower
in Public Gardens
where peacocks open their thousand eyes for us
and birdpeople move noiselessly
through the dripping palmhouse
feeling your body under me
warm and alive as the grass under our feet

I LOVE YOU

When listening to Brückner in the sunlit bathroom
When the hills and valleys of your morning body
are hidden from my gaze by BodyMist
When I don't have to ask who it is on the telephone
When we can't wait till the programme finishes
When I slip out quietly leaving you to sleep
untroubled dreams till morning in your darkened room
When I walk out into the dark shining streets
bright signs from petrolstations lamplight on leaves
hard unyielding lights from city flats

I LOVE YOU

Walking home yellow moon over the rooftops
cars crawling girls stopping everywhere smelling of you
Going off to sleep still smelling the rich luxury lather in your
                                                           hair
Walking holding your mini-hand
Standing in the Saturdaymorning bank
hot with people worrying about money
Seeing half a bottle of gin smashed on the pavement
Even when seeing schoolgirls on buses
their blackstockinged knees in mourning for their lost
                                                      virginity

I LOVE YOU

On trains
in cars
on buses
in taxis

I LOVE YOU

in that midnight hour
when all the clocks stopped
and it was midsummer
forever.

Holcombe Poem/Poem For a Girl I Didn't Meet

walking on the moors thinking about how I didn't meet you
                                                    yesterday
heather underfoot and mist over Pendle
the moor changing like an animal/brown to green grey to
                                    purple with the weather
sky blue at the edges
                        like a letter that came too late

*. . . Undine rising from the waters her golden hair
dripping in the moonlight . . . dead bird on a fence blood
dripping from its neck . . . Isis searching in the rushes
for her murdered lover . . . small girl with a fishingrod
in a rushing valley full of ferns . . . the last supper
followed by the Four Just Desserts . . . watching the
white mocking figure at the edge of the Dark Forest
. . . beating naked blondhaired girls with
longstemmed purple flowers . . . Osiris judging
the dead mist rising up the valley seaweed tangled
in her moonlight hair . . .*

trains
        moving through valleys
chimneys
        springing from hillsides
streams
        tumbling through boulders
clouds
        tilting from the horizon
and
    me
        on the moors
thinking about the girl I never met.

Remember

And somewhere
it will always be Whitsun and summer
with sandals to keep the rain from your sunburnt feet
And you will have just given me a bunch of artificial flowers
lilies-of-the-valley made of cloth with stiff glossy leaves
And turn and wave goodbye smiling
hair over your eyes caught in sunlight by the windowframe
. . . Remember?

ANSELM HOLLO

Stop Saying Oh, Oh

arm's length
and a half
from where I am: you

I can't see you

under the breastbone I am,
unable to hear you
for the continuous trembling

snake, biting its tail

'words, chatter
don't help the sick nor cure them'

but holding you   gives back a voice
and at least half a mind
                          mine, I suppose

        breathing,
trying to think of the lights
                          (love) lights

Bear Love

1 *for ever and a day*

thinking of how I am always
'a long way from home'
and looking for a bear   to take me to the mountain
the glorious city inside the mountain
where all the lost people go

I remember how the one side of the record went on playing,
two hours   not turned, nor repeating itself

that was in the heart of the mountain

2 *the bear*

it was an old dance, and he took a few steps
he was surprised to remember
then stopped   gazing at her
his body felt huge and warm
he did not want to go on   but he liked the tune
                              she was the tune

3 *after you've gone*

the bear sat down
he felt weak   unable to move
his mind was going so fast
he fell asleep
his mind was going so fast

The Days: Air

the riddles I talked in
when I saw you again

I wanted
                I was
shy
      to touch you

        . . . my hand
on your waist as it moved
beside me

walking
this part of town
that part of town

'I like
        this part of town'
said the English-
man, 'this is
much nicer than that other
part of town I mean
where we just were'

                        he tended
to fall on his face

while I was walking,
held
      by your eyes

and the sun pouring down

the puzzles we solved
in the evenings

I raise my hands
to have them remember,
tracing you
               in words & air

L'Indienne

fuzzy with light round the edges
  you were, as

    you sure that wasn't just your eyes?
     you said

      maybe
    but then they were
      my eyes

       as you came walking, as

      Most-Beautiful-Day

Poem

it is a poem
but is it   the trewf? says the daughter

it is (he said
somewhere inside)
that so many things
tho' not here   are true

Battersea Power Station
for instance   and you

the proof   the trewf?
in the thinking, the loving

fire and heat and smoke
and the light
at the ends of the grid

our fingertips   touching
lit up those days

MICHAEL HOROVITZ

Direct Communication
(poet to secretary)

why paint your mouth
that pillarbox red
if you don't want
my letters popped in—

only mail can be expressed
with any degree of certitude
as to its delivery
to another

but I tell you I love
you don't you
understand I'm crazy
about the way you lick

stamps

Dawning

Clearly   now yes now
so dearly   I know you
—not through and through
not yet   but through
your body   and your mind
the exact way   you wind
a thread around
   your index
finger   —brush your hair
and teeth   frenziedly
—sniff the air
secretly   save your fare

—I sense   your heart
movements   way
down in your soul
up with your dreams
   a stone fell
your hopes
screams   mad mopes
and innocently
diabolical schemes

—arrays
soap   milk   fruit
cheese and wine
to dine and determine
matters fine
—curious   to prepare
and discover
reveal   for another

—Not mine
own person—how possess
but share   recline
let beauty bless
you   lover
mother   wife
spell life

and   no going back
but let what
   we withheld
come   forward now
   dawn glow
and light the years
   ahead

I can see you
   groping
   against yourself
your features fold
   stern in concentration
—hear your voice
squeal in passion
smile in calm
—feel the agony
of your cunt   your balm
   of life-creation

—It's not because I know
you can cook
   you'll suit me to a
   budding tree
I do—

Because
  the way you look
  you are
and sing   laugh   cry
and cast your dye
your ecstasy
  and your denial
of self   and others rights
  for every law
to rest in peace awhile
at land's end

  and savour
each flavour   rock
salt   sea
  the hard
and the soft   sweet
sabbath   early
birds   mass

—because of how
you delicately
eat and drink   and tend
the sink   the sick
and   most happily
—the well

Your concern for pots
and lots of space
for content
and for surface
Oh—how you're
much too young
for lace
  a baby cries

why why
Yes I
   want to wake up
every day   and kiss
your face   your breast
your neck   and face
the world   with you
love   curled
in my arms

and carry our children
on my shoulders

For My Wife and Chagall

   When our two bodies
are lain to rest

our spirits fly straight
up the sky

   We gave to the world
one another's best

and gave up wondering
how the wind

forces the candles to pray

MAURICE COCKRILL

Spangle

We must climb over
the rocks and boulders
she said,
and she was so lovely.
I was trying to listen,
in my mind lines with
Solidary and Solitary
and hearts being
lonely hunters even.
Then we jumped a rope
into the pitted sand.
I'd felt like this before,
and so had she.

This feels like my home,
she whispers gliding
through the ghosts,
and clouds the corridor
with a wreath
of glinting dark hair
that coils at the tips.
And the music came
out of the ceiling.

You must never have a dream,
Because if you have a dream,
You're gonna have
A dream come true.

Under the loveyouforever bed
the egg-timer lay
on its side,
she in one flask
me in the other,
sifting dust.

Park Trip

Coloured and numerous
Wandering comets fall
Red for green
Letters
From a young smooth lip
Crusading through
Volumes of new fields and trees
Tracing the fitful maps
Of my comic romance.

FRANCES HOROVITZ

For M

This tree
leaned its green light
against our window
all last summer long.
Leaves budded and grew
precise as number
proliferate as stars.
In this green firmament
we saw the wind move
and the sun's stipple
on the earth below.
From taproot to the twig
of blackbird's perch
we knew the nerve of life,
knew in our veins
this sap of love
that reached towards the sun.
Leaves danced as we danced.
We sang the birdsong in the cage of air
and learned, through this,
our winter solstice, longest night,
bore growing seeds towards the light.

Morning Waking

casually perfect
    as a leaf or shell
upon white sheets you lie
emblem and cipher of yourself

your lineaments are royal
    as those of ancient monarchs
        upon coins

and as remote
    as those dead kings
        from my seeking eye

Loving You

soft as old silk
I tread in this room
wary of space
that between us flows
you know me
as fish knows fish in tide—
no more you know
I could mark you through to the bone—
no touch
you'd own
so gently I walk
around the space
enclosing you
soft as silk
loving you

ROGER McGOUGH

The Act of Love

The Act of Love lies somewhere
Between the belly and the mind
I lost the love sometime ago
Now I've only the act to grind

Brought her back from a party
Don't bother swapping names
Identity's not needed
When you're only playing games

High on bedroom darkness
We endure the pantomime
Ships that go bang in the night
Run aground on the sands of time

Saved in the nick of dawn
It's cornflakes and then goodbye
Another notch on the headboard
Another day wondering why

The Act of Love lies somewhere
Between the belly and the mind
I lost the love sometime ago
Now I've only the act to grind

Comeclose and Sleepnow

it is afterwards
and you talk on tiptoe
happy to be part
of the darkness
lips becoming limp
a prelude to tiredness.
Comeclose and Sleepnow
for in the morning
when a policeman
disguised as the sun
creeps into the room
and your mother
disguised as birds
calls from the trees
you will put on a dress of guilt
and shoes with broken high ideals
and refusing coffee
run
alltheway
home

The Icingbus

the littleman
with the hunchbackedback
creptto his feet
to offer his seat
to the blindlady

people gettingoff
steered carefully around
the black mound
of his back
as they would a pregnantbelly

the littleman
completely unaware
of the embarrassment behind
watched as the blindlady
fingered out her fare

. . . . . .

muchlove later he suggested that instead
ofa wedding-cake they shouldhave a miniaturebus
made outof icing but she laughed
andsaid that buses werefor travelling in
and notfor eating and besides
you cant taste shapes

There's Something Sad

There's something sad
about the glass
with lipstick on its mouth
that's pointed at and given back
to the waitress in disgust

Like the girl with the hair-lip
   whom
      no one
        wants
          to
            kiss.

CARLYLE REEDY

these poems are of love

the open wind
slacks
          to rough

the even ground

it is difficult
to know just what

have i found
          ?

          both
          read
each on each
                    side

our room has only one
          perhaps a hundred

Watt
light

two bodies   root
                  their beginning
     earth

   beneath the blanket
                    field covering
  even the quickness of trees

i was thinking of something
              your hair
                   it flies in the wind
i was   thinking   something

         dearest .

      gone   to shoot   pool .
        see you
   there .

ALAN JACKSON

The Emperor's Despatch

come to me tonight
on flowering feet
this meeting drags
and I don't care
about their troubles on the bloody border
two furry tribes have taken a stone town
   and my generals are mad
   to go and slay
but my mind is closing from them while they talk
I almost feel I can feel your legs
  and see your witty tits

I remember the first time I saw you dancing
and thought: That I fancy
easy for an emperor except
too easy and never knows
what he wins his women with
gold and the left-hand seat
or what

so I never made the usual summons
for you to come and know
what was expected
for rumour to reach fact
and you be famous
for a few nights' work:

how long will this thing last,
the little bitch?
with tiny breasts
and northern hair?
long enough to make her worth a visit?
or shall we wait
till he wakes tired?
again

but I kept your father here
in search of business
and found out ways to meet as you passed
by the river or in the garden walks
to let you see I lingered on your looking
and was waiting for your shyness
                              or your smile
until we talked
as if I was not the key to towers and kingdoms
and you were not being honoured by a glance

and now that we've both known each other naked
and I have thrown a vase just missed your head
and you have run away all grim and pouting
and I never sent to get you from your aunt's
   I know my cloak's just cloth that hangs on shoulders
that my crown is just a hat that makes me great
that you are half my empire and my equal
and that soldiers kill and conquer on tired feet

so anyway I'm sending you this letter
(they think I'm making notes on their campaign)
      come tonight
      for sunset walk in garden
      wear your blue and yellow
      and stay mine

I Only Kiss

I only kiss
a girl
can heal
the scissored nerves
inside my skull.

That's few.

Result,
when I do,
is destruction
for two.

Here's to the Girl

here's to the girl who stands up straight
and lies down so
no faiths no fears no promises
we come and we go

Hat

Nothing in my woman's head
didn't worry about that
Took her in to C and A's
and bought her a great big purple woolly hat

Edinburgh Scene

we used to be typists
but the hell wi that
now we live with these boys
in a two room flat

we've never washed for ages
we sleep on bits of sack
we've baith lost wir pants
and we dinnae want them back

the boys are a' big beardies
they think we're awfy sweet
we never know which one we're with
that's what it means to be beat

PETE MORGAN

The White Stallion

There was that horse
   that I found then
   my white one
big tall and lean as
   and mean as hell.

And people who saw me
   would stare as I passed them
   and say
     'Look at him . . .
   how he rides his cock-horse.'
But my steed
   the white stallion
stormed into the moonlight
   and on it was me.

There were those girls
   that I found then
   my loved ones
small fat and lean ones
   and virgins as well.

And those girls who saw me
   would weep as I passed them
   and cry
     'Look at him . . .
   how he rides his cock-horse.'
But my steed
   the white stallion
went proud in the still night
   and on it was me.

There was one girl
    that I loved then—
    a woman—
as tall and as lithe as
    a woman should be.

And soon as I saw her
    I dismounted my stallion
    to stay
        by the woman
    whose love I required.
But my steed
    the white stallion
rode off in the moonlight
    and on it was she.

Goodbye to the horse
    to the woman
    and stallion
farewell to my cock-horse
    and loving as well.

To people who see me
    and stare as I pass them
    I wail
        'Look at me . . .
    I once rode a cock-horse.'
But my steed
    the white stallion
is lost in the moonlight
    and on it rides she.

My Moll & Partner Joe

As my Moll & Partner Joe were stepping up to leave
the old black witch from somewhere else was tugging on my
sleeve
she was chanting spells above my ears and talking down her
hat

words about fidelity and the welcome on the mat
but my Moll & Partner Joe they were treading up the stair
there were flowers growing in his eyes and water in her hair.
The cardboard hard man troubled me—he was going to insist
on holding up my fingers and bunching up my fist
but my Moll & Partner Joe they were dancing in the street
rainbows round their fingers and wings about their feet.
The iron fairy shuffled in—her halo round her eyes
she bore machineguns at her breasts and bombs between her
thighs

but my Moll & Partner Joe they were far too gone to miss,
bolting up his parlour door they knew no more of this.
My gentle mistress welcomed me with garlands at her gate
I was bearing wreaths already and there was no time to wait
for my Moll & Partner Joe were by now being indiscreet
plucking ivy from the bedsprings—roses from the sheet.

ROGER JONES

The Snow Which Fell Last Year
(for Ofelia)

Love came in the door
and went out the window

He was busy and
didn't notice
until later

He lifted his head

Something was different
only—
it was too late

He got up and closed the window
bolted the door

and sat down again
to wait
his head on his hands
listening

for music outside the door

for wings beating
on his window-pane

For Betsy

everything was only
pictures on a screen until
you came along

    —clipclop
    —clipclop

a fork to my spoon

Because

simply because you were
young and perhaps not far from
beautiful
for a time i loved you in my way
along with a hundred other
anonymous
possibilities

Lesson

I have learnt
one thing about love—
You cannot possess the citadel
from the outside

PETE BROWN

Four Colour Poems

I

As red
as those leaves
in death / is your hair
alive

II

Pink—
well,
lips.

III

—and a green dress once /
very short / almost caused
a highstreet jam
in broad daylight
between friends

IV

Gold faded mixed with blue
journeys finished forgotten
arrangements postponed, begun again
an empty flat/new cars, a train
travelposter girl on a strange beach
with the sun
or someone

Shaken

Shaken by love
waking in the dark
tried to switch on
a vase

Skies

My sky is full of office windows
Your sky of snow clouds
I will draw peaceful aeroplanes
on yours
If you will draw the curtains
across mine

Springpoem in Glorious Colour
(to Jane Asher)

You are like the good times
when sun shines
into brown glooms
and blossoms whisper,
Yes, yes, a young tree . . .
red sky fire
a face moving slowly
in all the sleepless
waves of dawn; behind windows,
puzzled gaze as cars pass
through your hair
on the way to possible
spring; but smile, ah,
there are such as you

MIKE EVANS

For the 200 Susans

You flew
    like the bird
    on the
soldiers button
    from the mountains
        to the river
where the bridges
        are broken
        and
    covered with grass

Walking silently
    in violent meadows
    you smelt
        of biscuits
        at teatime
and your feet made noises
        like November
            bonfires

Crying
    when you first
        saw blood
        on the moon
you went out
    and collected flowers
        for lonely children

Painting my backyard
with wine
and smiles
you threw kisses
to the blind musician
next door

You said goodnight
and the judgement
of the silent jury
carried on
through the empty
daybreak streets
forever.

Poem

The morning rain
as we laughed
across streets
waking up.

The sunlight kisses
all over
your body
at dawn

The summer tears
as we said goodbye
through
the angry crowds.

Blues

My baby left me
    the other day
left my plaster room
    and naked lightbulb mind
left my lifetime blues
    at the eleventh bar

Left me to fight
    the midnight hour alone
left wildflowers to grow
    around my bed

Ended the poetry
    of our whispered conversations
ended the boogie-woogie strut
    on ivory beaches.

The Girl in the Long Yellow Nightgown

the girl
in the long yellow nightgown
        laughed at
the way I spoke /
        told me about
somebody
I always wanted
to meet /
        took me in
to all
her hidden
palaces of fire /
        waved goodbye
through wine
and smiles
and miles
of stoney stairways.

LIBBY HOUSTON

Since You Sir Went Away

1. A Game of Statues

channelled in a single
artery, we slashed it
& the streams flew out

but the baking air
stole their speed away

& now across the trough
they stare at each other
two flat snakes of clay

2. Booth

the puppet has lost its strings

on the sand a bundle fallen
from a hollow petrified shaft

wait for the south wind
& see if it moves!

3. Eyeing

I looked at the sun
eye to eye to find
the pit white
an unsounded sea of knives

4. Boots

he stamped out the flame

& who gave you the tongs you used
to set tongue-blemished branches,
black, on my plate?

here is an answer to play with:
the fire is dead

5. Desert

the limits of that time curved in:
closed brackets clenched tight
& too rusted to wrench apart for room
to sink a promised well

6. Careless Song

good bye gone winter
blow my hat to sea
(but he was not a bastard)

the weed will carry him
a green fever cry
the shark
can rake his eyes
(but he was not a bastard)

One Table, Two People

There are no words on either side
not one summonable to mind—

But! there is continuous air,
philosophically taking care,
to & fro like a swingboat at the fair

Flesh-&-bloody sense-data provide
the jabbering freight that rides

Light Music

The sun sat on top of the maypole
  & willows bandied the heat
while I did spring among dandelions
  along with my bare feet

come with me there now I'm
sorry you brought night but—
there'll be owls figure-skating,
& hedgehogs, licking the moon—

Poem

Ugly pollards beginning to shake,
  bright green and possessed:
You Are My Wind-break—
  you, stand up! (I'll rest).

Necklace

Here is a necklace for you

Shut your eyes—
What do you feel?

I have strung
the coldnesses of my tongue

RICHARD HILL

Photograph of Vivienne

You sit
in yesterday's sunshine
smiling
eyes tight against the sun
while motionless
the trees
solid behind you
rest against the sky
and I
never knew you then

I was in other pictures
posed against other trees
smiling my petrified smile
at no-one
until now

And now
I am jealous of
photographs like these
taken before I knew you

your long hair golden
snatching at the sun

Yesterday Girl

I remember her face (I think)
and a summer evening
standing on the shore
watching the Mersey
turning in its sleep
and the seagulls crying
sliding down the sky
like kids on banisters
while we wrote
I love you
in the sweaty summer sand
with sticks
and skipped across rocks
and both held hands
to keep from falling
out of love

But we couldn't

Mrs. O'Neill
(A Tale of Unrequited Love)

Every evening
Before she went to bed
Mrs. O'Neill said
Goodnight
To that nice announcer
On her small T.V.
Because she was eighty
And very much alone

And when she died
He never even went
To her funeral

PETE ROCHE

Poem for Whoever

You ask me for descriptions: hear this music.

She is like the sorrow bird, taking
All tomorrow's rain
That I might see through windows to
A starfall of tranquility. She inhabits fawndreams,
Speaks with birds for comfort. Like the walking wind
She is all to me, shaping her lips
Against my fears. I need her silent moving mouth,
Her soft-strung shadows, her eyes again.
I try to draw from memory, but stolen sorrow
Keeps its fingers to my crystal knife.
Let me say this—that I might speak like echoes
But only she can sweep the memory of midnight
From my eyes.
Hesitant in words, she speaks
With all her movements, offering herself
Without self-pity, making my fears seem like
My transgressions. Flowing from her gentle torment,
Watching her, my eyes assume
The bright green glass of rivers, flooding
Outwards, to the mouth of longing.
Knowing her naked, without her I would be
Beyond despair.

Old, Old, Story

The brief fly-buzzing building spirals
In the room's one silence, it occurs to me
That it's a strange reversal of
The ways of nature
For a fly to spin a web.
Stranger still—having spun—to
Step inside (mindful of precedents) to
The beautiful enchantress, waving
Her eight wiles. Yet I cannot complain
(Struggling hopelessly in this heart-woven web)
If she proceeds to pluck out both my wings
With disinterested precision,
Making it impossible—were it not
Already so—for me to
Fly away.

I shall
Crawl from her, side
Ways, down
      this
          broken
              pain.

Somewhere on the Way

I wanted to say a lot of things:
I wanted to say how often lately
Your bright image has wandered through
The dusty old antique shop of my mind;
I wanted to say how good it is
To wake up in the morning
Knowing that the day contains
Something that is you.

I wanted to say a lot of things:
I wanted to talk about
The changing colour of moments,
The silent secret language
Of bodies making love.
I wanted to say that you
Are always only as far from me
As thoughts are from thinking;

I wanted to say
I love you
In fourteen foreign languages
But most of all (most
Difficult of all) in English.

I wanted to say a lot of things,
But they all seem to have lost themselves
Somewhere on the way; and now I'm here
There's nothing I can say except
Hello, and
Yes, I'd like some coffee, and
What shall we find to talk about
Before the night burns out?

Connections

Missing the bus to Hammersmith
Means you miss the train to Leicester Square
Which means in turn (and following
The ghastly business to its
Logical conclusion) that you miss
The overnight express
At Euston;
A kind of chaos that will not stand
Over-close inspection
(The name of the game is Connections)

Naked in darkness, fumbling, tumbling
Together, any minute now one or both of us
Will burst out laughing, and as for me
I'm all for leaving the light on, but
The meter's just gone—which
Being so, we fumble on, quite unaware
That we are, in fact,
Pushing in
Different directions
(The name of the game is Connections)

Words like Hello and Goodbye sound much the same
When spoken from the bottom of a well;
It's hard to tell whether people are singing
Inside their heads; beds creak louder
In the dark; missing the mark
Is worse than missing trains.
Naked in cities, tumbling, fumbling for
Friends, regretting the way love tends to lead
To logical rejections (And the name of the game
Is Connections).

SPIKE HAWKINS

Waif

Accept this thin thread of sound
And nearness to a bed in summer
Whose soft heat stays in half filled
dresses
As the smell of women is the climates
and ageing of small planets to be found
in wardrobes inhabited by scents and falling
Of that which is carried and can easily be lost
From that dress summer grew
and legs that leaned from trunk threw out the
soft brown of the head and crept in with colours
to be distilled from lightness
And the body has its own ocean for its smiles
to float on

Lucy

In rooms draughts moor fingers
to the sight of her smiling to
sleep
Whose weather fans the snow propellers
of her body
And they fall down season

Excitement

Smiles like cigarettes can be enjoyed in bed
It depends on how you like your ornaments tonight
with tickets for all the flights
    I lie down to sleep with you
    Little with night
Eyes breaking into brittle animals

Poem

My machine sits in front of me. I am alone on
a bench. Soon she will come to me in a standing
door. Oh why do her hands and arms lie helpless
at her sides. It is the trembling earth and
flying stones that lie about us. If I say to
her, she stares as I kick in the waters of her
eyes. A flowing in clothes and small patches of
warmth when I touch her body. So unexpected the
surfing greens in evening fingers that grew smoke.
And looking up to trees, we fell from them to
land ourselves again. The slowing peopled evening
and its comings and going, register poor heads,
poor heads, poor heads.

Nest

The giant bird has left the attic
Alone the attic empty
Neat no longer a nest in the pillows
You're not there
The bird has flown
The bird has no longer a weekend
We are alone
The life is dry in the room
As a garden whose little girl
swims with the cat into the pool
Onto a plain of poplars full of all
the times you reached the cinema
and found the bird in the front
row in love with the ice cream dragon

TED MILTON

The Lockup

It is not so much
chrome handle

as crowbar
to bludgeon marauders.

Irresistible,
the beautiful body.

So he has fitted her up
with brilliant devices

which ring a little bell
in one of his thighs

if ever the cell
should take fright.

That ray of light
is his special delight,
in all weathers.

In My Lady's Chamber

Your room & I can't hear the ebb & flo of motors or the
        invading musics or the clock,
We've ears only for the click-click of high heels down in the
        street,
We're waiting solely for one pair of lady's shoes to come to a
        stop just below because then we'll know it's you
Arrived home filling the staircase with echoes of footsteps
        keying the lock shoving the door
Coming nearer & nearer down the corridor towards us basket
        brushing against the wall
A moment's pause the suspense! to wonder whether there's
        anyone here inside but as the handle turns
You've made up your mind you blow in you smile the door
        clicks shut
The wind's given herself up the warm & gentle wind
Don't move don't make a sound
Forever together
Silence.

Psalm

My windbreak
in winter

My shadow
in summer

Hung Up

Sometimes the line's died
between our eyes.
What's the matter?
you've said.
Nothing
I've replied.

Sitting there motionless
with heads bent
nursing our lives—

love's wilderness.

CAROLE SENIOR

Asleep You Touched Me

In the reaches of the
    escaping night
You reached for
    daisy dreaming
    long haired
    goodbye to mother
    me
Pulled me into the
    nook of
        was it Bill or was it Ben
        songsoft lustrous goodnight eyes
    your neck
Where on your flesh
    I felt the hundred me's
    gone before,
    gone transient flesh
    remain dark shadows
    clawing their way
    towards me with stealth and sharpness
    over the precious white of your skin
And winged doubts flashed loudly
    in the wardrobe,
    tin cans jangled sweet words,
    your masked face embroidered
    on the pillow
    was a feather, full and fanciful
    just afloating

on the breeze.

Winter Wedding

Damien doesn't cry
Damien collects dead leaves
on a golden afternoon
Cloud faces stuck on the sky
like postage stamps the wrong way
watch Damien
crushing the leaves
in his thick short fingers
lining his pockets
with brown confetti
saved for a winter wedding
And years ago the trees
were just the same
standing by without a word
While birds played swings
and roundabouts
in their boughs
And Damien's pockets bulge
with flakes of leaves
saved for a winter wedding
to float tears over the
Autumn-gone bride
flustering in belled air

Crisp in the crisp air
Damien doesn't cry.

Disunity

You turned
and in a moment
I saw your eyes
And I wanted so much to hold you
But I didn't.

You rose
and suddenly there was so much
I wanted to say
But I couldn't.

You left
and the gulf between us
      widened
I looked at the door
      stopping the evening sun
Then the window
      watching it
And I wanted to slide to you
on the fast fading light.

GEOFF HILL

Unable to Move

You lie there
with your set mouth and your fixed stare
disturbing me with that purposeful look
which I have learned to fear.
I know that you will be unable to move
till you know that you are going somewhere.

'Listen!' you say as outside our window
in the warm night Spring impinges
upon the sensory perceptors of some bird
and it sings of nothing in full-throated ease.
'Listen!' you say 'a nightingale
is calling for its mate.'

You lie there even now
with your set mouth and your fixed stare
printing your purposes on all that come before you
as if they petitioned your eyes and your ears
with their purposelessness
and begged your tongue for reasons. . . .

Maybe things could have been better.
We are unable to make more than love.

I always thought you could never miss
what you never had
forgetting how bitterly you might miss
what you thought you had
forgetting how you could still believe
what they told you in school

and that you might insist
that they couldn't have been lying.

But now I have told you that I have nothing to show you
except what I might have
and I have nowhere to take you
except where I might go.
And when you say 'Look! the trees seem
to be stretching out their branches to the sky!'
I write you wicked poems
telling you that they are blind
and they are pressing their way where they can
like slow forked lightning
where the air offers least resistance
guided only by the faint braille of the wind. . . .

The Gift

Girl
with your eyes like some creature
quivering
in slight sunlight
you come before me
speechless
like my own symbol of peace

always in your hands
some gift
which I will always take
taking your giving
less readily
than your gift

you seeming
as if you yourself
want to be more and more
of me.

Sad Girl

They tell me you are wandering now
with your eyes downcast and looking pale—
   pale as a lily, someone said.

All the blood from your never-so-pale cheeks
is drawn in to your pale pink heart
   which occasionally beats.

And your petals, they say, are drawn about you
(you do not like the sun)
and you do not even open at night
although you are now a student of the sky
   and possibly infinity.

They say you have never looked so sad before.
I have not seen you but I am sure
that you have never looked so beautiful
   have you?

On a Train

You can't say she should have told you.

She didn't know.

You should have known.

This has happened before.

You haven't learnt a thing.

You pathetic bastard standing there in front of the mirror trying to figure out what went wrong think about the bad times the jokes she flattened the points she missed the utter now you realise it STRANGER you must have been kissing all those times and places during your gentle strangler's overtures to his nighttime's hotblooded multiple murders.

Yes—you remember—but it doesn't help
to realise that you have really lost nothing
and that you are no worse off now.
It was an illusion
but at least you were really fooled.

When you went whoring home each night unable to stop you fondled every house down every street drank in everyone's night air as if it was all really free made love to their lawns leaving front gates wide open behind you regardless of the possible consequences and your breath steaming over their windows and your love all over the crazy paving and down the road and through the town not caring that anyone might follow you because you were guilty of nothing except giving and giving and giving. . . .

Now you are sitting in a railway carriage
opposite the beautiful girl in pink shoes
who got in at the last station.
The trees and houses sweep by
glistening in the sunlight
after rain.

This should please you.
It would have then.

The train is moving for you.
Somebody else inside you is doing your screaming for you.
You sit there with the Children's Crossword
scribbling words in the newspaper margin. . . .

We go underground at Baron's Court.

RICHARD SYLVESTER

Electronic Baby

Electronic baby,
Let me test your circuit,
Let me take your valves out one by one,
Blow on them,
Polish them,
And replace them all
Individually.
Let me trace your wiring,
And apply solder
To each of your aching connections.
Let me plug you in
To the direct current
Of my desire.
Let me switch you on
With calm precise movements
And explore the full range
Of your dial.
Let me, with full amplification,
Tune you in to Radio Prague,
Garner Ted Armstrong,
And the Third Programme,
Simultaneously.
Electronic baby,
Let me finally come
Into your closed circuit.

Mrs. Jones

Mrs. Jones likes jasmine tea.
I liked Jasmine when we met,
A slender girl with auburn hair
Who laughed a lot and danced a lot,
And killed herself one day at three.

Mrs. Jones likes steaming baths.
Jasmine used to bath with me,
And stroked me as I dried her legs
And held me as we went to bed,
But drowned herself one day at three.

Mrs. Jones can't swim at all.
Jasmine swam all day at sea;
We once raced to that bay and back
(But flat-irons tend to drag you down—
They dragged down Jasmine once at three.)

Mrs. Jones can paint with oils.
Jasmine carved in ebony.
She carved my head in oak-wood once,
And laughed because the ears stuck out,
Then slipped into a lake at three.

Jasmine was missing thirteen months.
They only found my Jasmine's bones.
She's paid her price (though what it was
She paid it for I do not know)
And I have married Mrs. Jones.

While the Glow Worms Sleep

While the glow-worms sleep
I will creep
Stealthily
To your room.

There,
Gasping,
Grasping,
We shall meet:

Custodian
Of secrets,
Keeper
Of mysteries

I shall
Wrest from you.
I will hear
Not-a-mouse stir,

Not your mother
Not-entering
This place
Of love,

Only
Your father,
Ire-full,
Rifle

Ready
To do battle
For your honour,
Unmindful

That I
Already
Have won
That war.

Poem

This morning,
Beneath the cracks
In the kitchen ceiling,
Watched by the stains
On the walls,
In spite of coffee
Spilled on the table cloth,
And burnt toast,
And broken promises,
In spite of
Many other reasons
Too numerous to mention,
And while a smashed chair
Looked on morosely,
You said you loved me.

Tonight
I shall fly to Rome
To have you declared
A bona fide
Miracle.

TONY JACKSON

For Carol (2)

shrouded in yellow
                    dressed in blue
crossing the bridge
                    in yr memory
                              thinking abt you
                    and waiting for yr
               return
silently remembering
                    not forgetting
          anything abt you
     remembering all that there is to know
               silently
               emptily
     not forgetting
     always remembering
          in my mind
                         in my brain
       soul heart
       sleep heart
                    rest in peace
          resting in peace
                         go you

For Carol (8)

she rises
lovely
from the deep

her hair that burns
the eyes that burn

turns her face
to the sky
clouds are passing
turns her face
to the sky
into clouds that are passing

see her rise
from the deep
eyes that flame

see the water sent
cutting from
her brain

she rises
lovely
from the deep

and
smiling
casts it
away

14 year olds
teetering round
on their first
hi heels

or madly flopping
hair falling over
new found breasts

flowered jeans
blooming around
their
sprouting mounds

& their eyes of
angels
will soon
die

PAUL EVANS

The Branches

A shower of birds fell
into the branches above us,
singing quietly at first
but louder as the evening rose to meet us.

Old men trooped out
from their houses
to sit at tables
under the branches.

Old women passed
in black clusters,
making small noises
with their teeth and ornaments.

Later, in the bedroom, in the hotel,
some certitude
of infinity
in the hand's length

between the woman's mouth and mine.
The eye of a bird
opening, and closing,
in the branches above the old men.

The Train
(for Rhiannon)

I

Heartbeat of the child
on the floor below

I want the rapid hollow drumming
of a steam train
shaking the window

Ealing: whistle of the great expresses out of the tunnel

Aberdare: crash of the black coal train,
shriek of its whistle

Cardiff: poignancy of the bucking cattle trucks
before I was born

the white steam
and the cinders flying,
               at night

2

Yes, I understand
the train,
the continual shunting
from siding to siding

the journey
returning me
out past the last cattle trucks,
beyond Cardiff

her face taking shape in a cloud of steam
she advances
out of the child's dream
into me
and we move together
gathering speed like the great expresses

we are one
in a blaze of
light and speed
we are coal and water
one piston
whistling out of the tunnel
into daylight
it is all speed
                    and motion

it is one direction

A Praise for Rhiannon

When my woman moves
                    she does not
break into a thousand pieces,
                            into air.

Her body is of earth
                    upright on beautiful
animal legs
like a creature of forests will stand
among trees
                quite silent,
                            one of them.

HEATHER HOLDEN

Love Poem

You are not my friend
suddenly
you are an ashen-faced pixie
lying under a Union Jack
with a blue bucket by the bed:

we were lovers
and I got up

the keys to your
room
are in my pocket

I wanted to make your bedside
a jungle of flowers

You can sit on the wing
of St. Francis bird
and get better

I would never throw away something
somebody loved

we are all separate
but it's not my doing

my friends and I are like chaffinches.

You Are a Creature

You are a creature—
that is beautiful that can sing,
you're a wood anemone
with green leaves,
you're a black cat
in a damp lane,
you're a creature
that is beautiful that can sing.
Like a bird on a twig
in the big blue dawn.

Summer Poem

I will bring you flowers
every morning for your breakfast
and you will kiss me
with flowers in your mouth
and you will bring me flowers
every morning when you wake
and look at me with flowers in your eyes

JOHN BROWN

Poem for Sherry

According to simple mathematics
Which I have studied assiduously
To O level
One Purple Aerosol of
Supersoft Hair Spray
For hard-to-hold hair
(With Perfume No. 3)
Does not equal
(Doesn't even come near)
One twenty year old girl
Small, most beautifully,
And once mine
For a very slight output
Of love, tender or otherwise,
(Maintenance minimal but fun)
And of caring, noticing &
Always needing in
Various tenuous ways.
Once mine/past tense.

This equation though
Perhaps on paper suspect
Contains the odd inevitable
Truth, as for instance
That my need for you
Will grasp, now that you've
Gone, at any small
Remainder, personal/impersonal
Thing you have left behind.
I am thinking surely

Somebody, perhaps a very
Poor somebody but still
Somebody, must have come back
Two hundred miles
For a four and
Sevenpenny Aerosol.

Once, now so long ago,
With a girl, we
Both sensing not
Long to go
Grabbing pieces of
Happiness too slowly
Everything fading dulling
She suddenly hugged me
Sniffed my neck, face,
Body, I not knowing
Asked why, she
Said smiling 'I'm
Making my memory'.
I have made too many memories
Even the wind will not blow them away

I cannot throw away
Those hastily-scrawled notes
You have, so often, left me
The notes about
'I've mended the things
Left them in the top drawer'
Who really expects me
To part with them?

Dreaming alone this morning
I touched the tips of your breasts
Painted finger prayers on your skin
You didn't move.
'Isn't there anything left?'

I pleaded with the
You of my dream
'No' you said,
Cruel for the first time,
You sneered
'I bet you wish you
Could say you love me'
Somehow it was the wrong
Way round.
I woke up screaming.

Like this, I have
Made too many memories.

Between the lights and
The shadows of us
Then & now
Between the lights and
Shadows of what is ourselves
(Secret selves will never fly)
There is a space
In which I cannot see clearly
Perhaps it is better
That I cannot distinguish
The point of merging
Of these shadows and lights.

Shadows, lights, tired,
Unthinking, too tired,
No, not like this,
Not these shadows
These shadow pictures
Not knowing
Will confuse my
Last remaining dove.
I must still try to fly.

Shadow light pictures
Too tired unthinking
No, not like this, for
I have climbed too many
Sad hills at dawn
Staggered hopefully up
Too many hilly city streets
Hiding from the sick morning lamplight.
I have climbed too many hills at dawn
With you beside me
Or wanting you beside me.
Even before I saw you
I wanted you beside me
At such times and others.

Why waste time talking
About blame or forgive?
That's not relevant
To my equation.
You have left me so much else
You have left me yourself everywhere
Every morning your body beside me
Your face open like a child's
And swollen with sleep
(We are only kissing truthfully
In our sleep)
You have left me
You walking beside me everywhere
You have left me
Yourself in every beautiful girl I pass
On crowded streets
And your face in flowers
Your touch through tears
Your hands in emptiness.
Shut in, I am unable to breathe,
Your face is everywhere

I cannot escape from you
Your face is everywhere around me
Ghosts I cannot leave behind.
I have made too many memories
Even the wind will not blow them away
I could not escape from you everywhere
Even if I wanted to.
Even if I should ever want to.

RAYMOND SALTER

Horse-lover

Finding I was one of a herd
I left for sake of
My respectability,
Leaving you to pace the
Ranks of horses' hooves alone,
Hoping that some day you
Might come by to see
Me grazing in a distant field:
There would be pleasant scenes
Of reunion, then
Forgetting all that's passed
We'd go riding in the wood.

Sure enough—out for air
One day without the rest
You saw me standing,

(I could not make a sign
For sake of my humility.)

I long for winter—
With this old rag of tail
I cannot keep the flies away.

Really There is Nothing to Say

Really there is nothing to say,
I have seen all that there is
To be seen of you
From head to foot
Uncoiled.

Stretched on the bed you lay,
I bit my nails,
There was a fly in the room,
And I remember odd things
Like a stain on the carpet,
The fact that your comb
Is always dirty.

We stayed like this for hours,
You on the bed
Me in the chair.

Towards evening it rained,
I opened the windows

It was late when you left,
The coffee cup half full,
Ash on the floor,
A trace of scent.

Journey

The pain of this slow progress
Which like a train crawls
Slowly through the suburbs
Of our love.

The spread of housing shutters
Off a vacant lot, an old car,
Broken bottles,

Through the empty station,
The seat in need of paint,

Down through tunnelled dark

You turn, I turn, we sit
Trapped between reflexions
In the glass.

BRIAN PATTEN

Into my Mirror Has Walked

Into my mirror has walked
A woman who will not talk
Of love or its subsidiaries,
But who stands there
Pleased by her own silence.
The weather has worn into her
All seasons known to me,
In one breast she holds
Evidence of forests,
In the other, of seas.

I will ask her nothing
And yet would ask so much
If she gave a sign—

Her shape is common enough,
Enough shape to love;
But what keeps me here
Is what glows beyond her—

I think at times
A boy's body
Would be as easy
To read light into;
I think sometimes
My own might do.

Party Piece

He said:

'Let's stay here
Now this place has emptied
And make gentle pornography with one another,
While the partygoers go out
And the dawn creeps in,
Like a stranger.

Let us not hesitate
Over what we know
Or over how cold this place has become,
But let's unclip our minds
And let tumble free
The mad, mangled crocodile of love.'

So they did,
There among the woodbines and guinness stains,
And later he caught a bus and she a train
And all there was between them then
was rain.

Song for Last Year's Wife

Alice, this is my first winter
of waking without you, of knowing
that you, dressed in familiar clothes
are elsewhere, perhaps not even
conscious of our anniversary. Have
you noticed? The earth's still as hard,
the same empty gardens exist? It is
as if nothing special had changed.
I wake with another mouth feeding
from me, but still feel as if
love had not the right
to walk out of me. A year now. So
what? you say. I send out my spies
to find who you are living with, what
you are doing. They return, smile
and tell me your body's as firm,
you are as alive, as warm and inviting
as when they knew you first.
                    Perhaps it is the winter,
its isolation from other seasons, that
sends me your ghost to witness
when I wake. Somebody came here today, asked
how you were keeping, what you were doing.
I imagine you, waking in another city,
touched by this same hour. So
ordinary a thing as loss comes now
and touches me.

Song of the Pink Bird

Let the pink bird sing; it's at your breast
In a room we're sharing
And your head on my chest confirms
Its glad domination.
Let the world play its games beyond the curtains,
We are certain of only one thing,
Let the pink bird sing.
We have lost interest in wars and political situations,
There are craters in our hearts,
We must not neglect them,
Let the pink bird sing.
Let it sing as long as singing matters,
Look through the curtains
The clouds are blushing,
The moon apologising—
Let the pink bird bring home to us
One reason for living,
Let the pink bird sing.

On a Horse Called Autumn

On a horse called autumn
among certain decaying things
she rides inside me, for

no matter where I move
this puzzled woman sings
of nude horsemen breeched
in leather,

of stables decaying near
where once
riders came,

and where now alone
her heart journeys, among
lies I made real.

Now riding in truth
what alterations can I make
knowing nothing will change?

Things stay the same:
such journeys as her's
are the ones I care for.

A Creature to Tell the Time By

I created for myself
a creature to tell the time by
   —& on the lawns of her tongue
flowers grew,
   sweet scented words fell
out her mouth, her eyes and paws were comforting—
   & woken with her
   at dawn, with living birds

humming, alien
inside my head,

I noticed inside us both
the green love that grew there yesterday
was dead.

TOM PICKARD

The Bodies Are Touching

What is the matter?

Where is your mind now?
What does it matter?

Something is sleeping
where the mind wanders

It wanders away
Let the mind stray

It gives back a pain
It sucks and is suction

The bodies are touching
                    touching

sandcastles built to smother you
with kisses on the nose and lips

sandcastles spread across the beach
by happy bathers

crumble my turrets with your toes,
wash me with your foamy sea,
make starfish my towers
whilst I bucket you with water.

Conny

Tears sealed behind your eyes
soak away your mind.

But last night when I thought you were asleep
your head soft between my breast and shoulder
I was about to stream the pillows with your hair,
to submerge into your flesh, caressing with my lips
your sensual parts
                    I felt a tear, and through the darkness
I could feel it shatter, streaming many ways.

To My Unborn Child

our heads met
when both of us
bent to kiss
your mother's womb
you
little bairn
bent on opening it

and I pressing it closed
with my lips

then I found
you had been there
all time, before me.

DAVID J. BLACK

Love Conquers All

All the world, we're told,
loves a love junky,
hooked by the flesh
on his one obsession
of the ideal romantic
entanglement prison
hungover with roses.
All is ignored
but the grand delusion;
and then,
bound in by the golden ring,
sadly discovers
that the love which moved mountains
now has to move prams.

Procreate

I see in dreams
countless reams
of possibilities;
thundering,
blundering
shower of light.
When I open my eyes
I realise
there's no possibility
but one,
and that's been done,
lying beside me now.

GILLIAN BARRON

Furniture
(A Song)

You made me furniture
marble gilt black leather
cardboard scenery
to furnish my dreams

I lived in a glass castle by the silver sea
in the ebony mountains trees sang like harps to me
for you were there, walking along behind me
in front of me and all around me

Then you went away, drove away
over the horizon at a hundred miles an hour
in an enormous navyblue removals van
laughing you robbed me of my furniture

Now I sleep under dustsheets in a warehouse
your thirtyseventh discarded lover in the corner
beaming foolishly as a standard lamp
The fridge is full of old stockings and a cold wind blows

Laughing you robbed me of my furniture
marble gilt black leather furniture
cardboard scenery
to furnish my dreams

Limbo River Autumn

time to wrap our daydreams in grey linen
and fling them to the weeds
and brown water

with the driftwood of a rainy summer in limbo
time to go in search of the leanflanked pike
that waits in the shadows of images

time to wade down the river of night
hand in pale hand
albino and leper; the otterhounds
follow close in the moon's trail

Romeo and Juliet

At midnight, when chimneysweeps
attack the sky, eyes glittering
a wind lifted them from the lamplit city
and, sharp-hooved over bony foothills, bore them
to a black swamp; they drowned.

Now he stands, watching her footsteps
fade from the shining sand
where she walks on the secret beaches
of islands asleep in the sea.